I0470979

Marketing Tips To
Catapult Your
Business to the Top
And Annihilate Your Competition

Eric Michael Roberts

ISBN-13:978-1490598246
ISBN-10:1490598243

CONTENTS

Introduction

Everyone wants more customers and more sales but it is hard work! You have to create and implement an effective and affordable plan. After years of trial and error, I have pinpointed 21 important strategies and tips to help you get more customers and keep more money in your pocket. The most expensive marketing is often the least effective marketing. Now you can stop guessing and use some of the techniques in this book to steadily grow your business and increase your sales. If you have ever wondered how to reach more people with the small budget you have available this book is for you! In the following twenty-one chapters, I will teach you how to attract new customers and get more sales.

My plan begins and ends with three simple

words: Know. Like. Trust. These three words are the driving force behind every technique I use. When people know you, like you and trust you, they will buy from you and tell all of their friends to do the same! My techniques will enable you to build an easy-to-implement system for marketing, which will result in customers that know you, like you and trust you. I will refer to this as the "Know, Like, Trust" factor.

Using these twenty-one techniques in my online and local businesses, I have made a very good income doing things that I absolutely love. Many months, less than 5% of my income goes toward marketing. This is much lower than the suggested industry standard for marketing campaigns but I want to keep more of my money so I only do what works and is affordable! I avoid traditional and expensive marketing solutions and I do most of the work myself. This approach works and is attainable for every hard working business owner. No matter what niche you are working in or what type of customers you have, you will increase your sales and customer base when you follow my proven techniques.

1

Web Site

You don't have to be the absolute best choice for the job, you just have to LOOK like the best choice and be visible when people are looking. Most people will judge your business in about 5 seconds when they see your web site for the first time. If you don't have a web site you will loose so much business it will be hard to stay in business. If you have a poor web site, you will loose a ton of business too. One of the best ways to get a flow of new customers and stay in business is to have a great web site. This in not a web design book so I cannot go into all the aspects of a great web site. I will, however, outline and describe three critical ingredients of an amazing business web site and explain a simple web navigation layout for successful service businesses.

Number 1:

You need to have a professional looking web site. If you are not a professional graphic designer (and most likely you are not) you need to hire a professional graphic and web designer to make your business logos and web site.

Number 2:

Your site has to be clear, concise and provide them with the most important information including prices and services offered.

Number 3:

You need a clear "Call to Action" on almost every page of your web site and especially on your home page. Most people will spend about 5 seconds on your home page before they decide if they will stay there or bounce off to another competitor's web site. You can loose a customer that quick! Decide what you are trying to get them to do and then quickly lead them to that action. It may be a phone call or a sign-up form. I include a specific call to action on almost every page of my web sites! Doing this keeps a steady stream of new customer and sales coming in.

2

Web Elements

One of the most important factors of a great web site is clear navigation and up-to-date information. An effective web site will include these pages:

HOME

Provide a bold call to action like "CALL TODAY!" This may be the only page they visit so make it simple, use good graphics and a compelling call to action. You want to provide a positive feeling and make sure you let them know you are highly qualified and in high demand. You should include at least one customer testimonial here and list some of your best and most visible clients. Provide links to your blogs, videos and other exciting content on the home page.

SERVICES

List your main services with clear prices. You don't have to list all of your services or products but include your most popular services, products and packages on this page

TESTIMONIALS

Put as many customer testimonials here as possible! Include a client list as well and be sure to update it often. When you work for a large client list them near the top and add a link to their business.

ABOUT US

Provide some simple information about you and your credentials to build the "Know, Like, Trust" Factor.

CONTACT US

Provide all of your contact information and a simple web contact form on this page. Let your customers know how you prefer to be contacted and how long it usually takes for you to respond. The more ways you provide the more likely they will be to contact you. Provide links here to your blog or your Facebook and social media pages and encourage them to connect with you.

You can view my actual business web sites to see how I use these techniques.

My web site at: www.pianotuningdayton.com is powered by wordpress.com. It is hosted FREE and it is very easy to configure. It is the main site that I use because it is easy to update and has easy-to-use blog features.

I also have this web site that I use to sell guitar lesson products:
http://www.8chords100songs.com

Eric Michael Roberts

3

Blog

This is a very important part of building your credibility and visibility online. It is easy to start a blog and will create a place online that you can share you knowledge and engage your customers. You can also share news, customer testimonials and write articles for your customers to read. Blogs index very well in search engines so this is one thing that will help you rise to the top in search engine results. I use my blog to share my successes and to give my customers relevant information. It is easy to set up a blog using wordpress.com or blogger.com. These are my two favorite blog engines. Blogs are free if you use the basic domain. You can easily set up a wordpress blog with a free domain that looks like this: yourbusinessname.wordpress.com

Be sure to add an article or update at least once each week. Every day is better but many people are to busy for this volume. Customize the look of the blog with your graphics and logos. With the wordpress engine, you can set up an entire blog that acts more like a web site. I use my blog as my main web site. I do this by setting up the navigation and pages to feel like a regular web site and it allows me to make frequent and relevant updates easily with and requires no code or web design skills. You can see how my blog/site works at www.worshiptheking.com

Link all of your social media sites like Facebook and Twitter to your blog and cross promote them.

4

On Top

It can cost a small fortune to be at the top of some categories in a national market but in most cases you can be on the first page for a reasonable amount. Using Google Adwords you can create a very targeted ad campaign to your customers and pay very little. Once you set your campaigns, monitor them daily until it is working perfectly. An Adwords campaign can take some time to manage but Google offers many tutorials and help along the way.

The goal is to have your web site showing up on the first page in your service area when someone is looking for your type of service. Some service industries are more competitive than others and your monthly budget will depend on the competition. I suggest setting aside one full week to research and read the google tutorials as you are setting up your first campaigns. Start with a low manageable budget and increase over time. Read some books on how to get the most out of the Adwords platform. Be sure to visit 21bookseries.com for some other great books to help you.

The greatest thing about this type of advertising is that you only pay when someone clicks on your web site and you are always dealing with a customer who is searching for your exact business and is ready to buy! There are other paid search engine programs offered including Bing and Facebook but Google is the most used and most effective. In the next chapter, I will discuss how to get your web site showing at the top of the organic (non-paid) search results. Both paid and unpaid are important and work together in many ways.

5

Organic Results

Getting on the fist page of any major search engine under the free or "organic" search results get complicated because you can't just start a campaign and pay to be on top. You only get to the top if you have a quality web site with a ton of relevant content. Using a few of these simple techniques, you can be on the first page and maybe even dominate the first few pages. This takes time and dedication but will help your business grow and can be accomplished even if you are not a computer genius. The most important factor is relevant content and links to your site from outside sources. You need to have a web site that is very focused toward your target market. Next, you need to have other web sites point to or link to your site. The more links you have from the outside pointing to your site, the more relevant your site will rank in search engines. The more relevant you are, the higher you are placed! For example, if your site is featured on the Wall Street Journal web site with a link, you will be perceived as important and get a higher rating than if you have a link from your friend's personal site. The trick is this: Get as many links to your site from big sites. How do you do this? Get reviews from the local newspapers, add links from your Facebook page, add links to your site from your Wordpress blog and keep getting other sites to add a link to your site.

Be sure to use relevant content within your web site. Make sure your page names are strong keywords and employ every SEO (Search Engine Optimization) technique you can find online and in current books. The more optimized your site is the higher it will rank in search engines. This process does not happen overnight and it is an ongoing process.

I discuss this in more detail in the next chapter.

6

Optimize Search

You don't have to be a web designer to be all over the web. First create a simple profile for your business with a few paragraphs about your services. Create a list of 10-25 top keywords that you suspect people will use when they are searching for your business. You should try the free Google keyword tool found   at https://adwords.**google**.com/o/**KeywordTool**

Then, find every listing service possible online and register your business. Sites like www.angieslist.com offer a great place to register your business. Create a profile on all the sites you can find. You should use craigslist and other listing services as well. Many of these sites are free and some offer a paid subscription. Create a Facebook page and Twitter Account. Also create as many other social media accounts as you can and link them all back to your main web site. Use your keywords and upload your company description and contact information to each of these sites. Provide links in every one back to your main web site. Create special blogs on various blog engines including www.blogspot.com, www.wordpress.com and others. Create a strong Google Plus Page and a Google Places Page. The Google Places Page is where you will link your paid advertising and will boost your organic results too.

Every listing site that points back to you strengthens your rank in search engines. Also, when a customer searches for your type of service, they will find you listed in multiple spots and you will begin to show up all over the first 1-3 pages of all the major search engines. This is a very important element of looking huge and being every place your customer clicks. Make sure that every listing directs your customers back to your main web site at www.Yourbusiness.com where you have a clear call to action and an online booking button!

7

Your Facebook Page

Facebook is a great place to connect with people. It is the largest social media hub online. I use Facebook to allow my customers to connect with me in a casual social environment. I do not rely on Facebook for a steady stream of new customers, but rather to build the know, like, trust factor. To be a part of Facebook, you will need to build a personal profile but the Facebook Page allows you to focus on your brand and your services/products. Post often and keep things interesting. I use trivia and run simple contests to get people engaged. For example: I ask a simple trivia question and give away a free pack of guitar strings to the winner. I pick the winners from the correct answers posted in the comments of that post. Post pictures of job or products. Post videos about your services. Post random facts that would be interesting to your niche.

You can invite your friends from your personal profile to "Like" your page. Be sure to add a "Like" button to all of your other web pages and even include it in your email signature. You can use the link from your facebook page to direct people to the page. Example: www.facebook.com/yourpagenamehere. You will need at least 25 "Likes" to pick a custom facebook URL. Once you get to that level be sure to pick something easy to type and remember. I create a custom banner for my Facebook page where I list my phone number and contact information. I have an online booking application that I use and include that on my Facebook Apps as well. (www.appointy.com).

8

Twitter

Twitter is very similar to Facebook but it moves much faster. It is made to post 140 mini status updates called "Tweets". You can link your Facebook and Twitter account so that they both update automatically when you make a post. The goal is to keep making Tweets every day. Most Internet marketing specialists suggest that you make at least five tweets every day! Follow people on Twitter that are similar to your brand or service and try to post engaging and personal tweets. As with Facebook put links to your Twitter page on all promotional materials and on every web page. Your twitter accont will be a simple link that looks like this: www.twitter.com/yourbusinessname. Use links to your products and services in your tweets and direct your followers to your web site as often as possible. You can tweet very casual things like: "I am hungry and need to order a huge pizza" or you can post updates about your business like: "Special 10% off coupon today only when you mention the word TREES at our store". When engaging in social media you need to open up and not take yourself so seriously. People just want a chance to get to know you. You can see my twitter account and follow me at http://www.twitter.com/8chords100songs

9

Email Newsletters

An email newsletter is a great way to stay connected with your customers without using stamps! When you send an email newsletter, be sure it includes fresh relevant content. Don't use the newsletter to keep asking for repeat business. This is used to build the "Know, Like, Trust" factor. Don't send emails too often. Depending upon your industry and content, a monthly newsletter is plenty of contact. If you send too many emails, your customers will opt out or report you for spam. The main reason you are sending this newsletter is to keep reminding your customers that you are there and to build a relationship. If you are not good at writing articles you can have a friend write for you or purchase articles for your niche from online writing services. You can even purchase complete newsletters for certain industries that are ready to print and send. I prefer to make my newsletters sound personal so I write my own content. I try to include a special coupon or offer for my loyal customers. I also include a personal story or highlight a recent job, testimonial or special business achievement. I use a great web service called www.mailchimp.com to send my newsletters. You can have up to 500 customers in your list and send emails free. If you have more than 500 customers, you will pay a small fee depending on the size of your email list. Another service that is very popular and easy to use is www.constantcontact.com.

10

Print Newsletters

To keep in touch and keep costs low, I send one yearly printed newsletter and a one custom Christmas post card to remind my customers that they are important to me. For the other monthly news, I use my email list as discussed in the previous chapter.

In this yearly printed newsletter, I write simple articles or news blurbs about the past year. I try to highlight a customer or a special artist that I tuned for that year. I sometimes, if applicable, add a coupon or a call to action for a special new service. I keep that part small and don't push for a sale. This newsletter is more about building relationships!

I use www.vistaprint.com to print and send my post cards and my newsletters. It is very simple to upload the client address list and design the post card using their simple design templates. You don't have to be a graphic designer to accomplish this. If you are uncomfortable with graphic layout and want to save money, your newsletter can be created in a simple letter from on your company letterhead.

11

Logos

A logo is a very important part of your brand. Once you create a great logo, you will use it on all of your print materials, flyers, invoices, business cards, web sites, social media sites and everywhere you promote your business. It is important that you make a logo that is easy to print and display on paper and the web. If you use a logo with full color photo graphics it can be difficult to make it look nice on a black and white letterhead. A great logo will include simple and unique colors and a graphic element that represents your business. Make your logo in high resolution and have it designed to pop of the page in color and in black and white. Make sure your name and your identity are clearly stated in your logo. Before you begin to mock up your logo design check out some national brands like Target and other national chains. You know that they have spent hundreds of thousands of dollars developing a look that will sell. Take cues from these large national brands and make your logo look like it cost a million buck.

If you are not a graphic designer it is easy to find one! You can have a nice professional logo designed by a freelance designer for $5-25 at http://fiverr.com/categories/graphics-design Fiverr.com is a great place to find special services to help you with the creative side or your business.

12

Print Materials

If you are not a graphic designer then please hire one! You can get a business design and logo package for a few hundred dollars. You will use these graphics for many years and you will look more professional if a professional graphic designer creates them. You can find these people by asking friends or other local businesses. If you do it yourself you run the risk of looking small and cheesy! Nobody wants to hire a small cheesy company. You need a great standout logo and a basic business card layout along with a letterhead and a custom sales receipt template. With these items in hand, you can have a local or online printer print all of your materials on high paper. I have found several online printers that stomp the local competition when it comes to business card printing and full color printing. I like www.gotprint.com

and www.moxicopy.com. They provide banners, business cards, receipt books, full color brochures and much more for up to 50% less than the local Kinkos.

If you are tight on cash and need to keep it simple, start out with a full color business card and a nice logo you can include in all of your other printed materials. www.vistaprint.com has nice business card templates you can use if you just cannot afford a graphic designer. Professionals designed the online templates and you can plug your information into the template.

If you skip this step you will never be able to compete with the larger companies in your service area. You need to look big and credible and your printed materials (along with your web site) will give people a good or bad first impression. If customers see your business card and think you are cheap or have poor taste they will throw it away and look for someone else. Always carry your business cards in your car and in your pocket. Be ready to pass them out and leave them with local businesses.

Always look at your competition and search

on Google for national companies to get ideas for your business logo and designs.

13

The Right Price

The first, but not most important, factor of making the sale is always going to be the "price factor". Setting the right price can make or break your business. Think about it… If you have the best product or service in the world but it costs too much, you will not be able to sell it. If you have an amazing product but charge too little you risk looking cheap and worthless. A higher priced item or service often looks more desirable but the price cannot be too high or you will price yourself out of the market.

Another factor that comes into play in the minds of the consumer is the "the great deal" factor. Most people will only make a purchase if they feel like they are getting a great deal. It is your job to create that illusion. They may or may not be getting a great deal, but you want them to "feel" like they just got a great deal.

The third and final factor is urgency! When the consumer feels that they need to make a decision right now, they are more likely to make the purchase. If you give them a window of opportunity to walk away and think about it you will probably never see them again.

I use these three factors: price factor, the great deal factor and urgency to get the cash flowing in my direction. Here is how it works. I set a retail price of $149.99. I then set a "limited time only" sale price of $99.99 IF they order today!

My retail price is set on the very high (almost absurd) side of what the market will allow. In other words, I find out what my competitors are charging and then I charge a little more! Then I run an urgent sale promotion, which makes my product cost a little less than the accepted normal or most visible competition. The final "sale" price needs to be an acceptable long-term price for you to sustain your business. The promotion is all about the psychology of the sale. I let my customers know that it's a limited time deal and then I ask them to take action RIGHT NOW! For example: Buy today and save $50. In my promotions I don't leave room for them to think about it very long. You can run an ongoing promotion like this as long as it comes across as urgent. You can say, "for a limited time only" or "while supplies last".

Try to structure your products and services using this model. It will most likely mean that you will raise your regular prices and then offer them "on sale".

Remember this: To the customer, the end price is less important than the feeling that they are getting a great deal.

14

In Sight

If you don't keep up-to-date detailed records, you will have a hard time building a long-term repeat customer base and you will be lost when you try to keep in touch with your customers. There are many services available for customer management. Choose one that will work on your computer and your smart phone and begin using it as soon a possible. I use Bento (www.filemaker.com/products/**bento**). It is an amazing system for me because I use a Mac and an iPhone. It allows me to create customer databases without any code and it syncs my information across my computer, iPad and iPhone. I set this up for under $100 and pay no monthly fees. There are other software and hardware options for Windows users and there are also online customer database options available. A quick Google search for customer database programs will get you started on your research. Before I switched my database over to the smart phone sync model as I just described, I would spend hours entering information from my field paperwork every week. Now I am able to create all of my notes and do my record keeping while I am on the job and it eliminates the need for extra paperwork. I can also recall my customer data in the field using my iPad or iPhone. You can view and download my bento template from the database I use on the FileMake web site at: http://solutions.filemaker.com/database-templates/detail.jsp?serial=2551724291

Filemaker provides a place for people to share their templates and custom database designs. I have shared mine there with other piano technicians around the world. It includes special data fields for all the important data that I want to track. You can make a database for your niche by drafting out the most important customer data on paper. I use a "notes" section to keep track of all the work that I have done for each customer. I also keep track of every communication that I have with them. This helps me remember who they are and how to approach them when I make a phone call.

Eric Michael Roberts

15

Feeders

You can pay thousands of dollars a year for a Yellowbook ad or fancy full color ad in your local newspaper but it will never pay off like having a reliable and loyal feeder network. What is a feeder network? It is a small group of loyal and similar businesses that refer you to their customer base on a regular basis. For example, as a piano tuner, I use private lesson studios as my main feeders. I call them feeders but they are really throwing me customers every week! Building these relationships takes time and you will need to prove yourself to them first, but the investment is well worth it. I give my special feeder network businesses a 40% discount on all the work that I do directly for them. When I work on their pianos, I spend extra time and I charge them considerably less than my standard rate. I explain to them up front that

I am giving them this huge discount because I rely on their recommendations. They quickly get the picture and they hand out my business cards (which I supply liberally) to all of their customers. Some of my feeder network businesses have over 400 regular students attending lessons every week. Every student has a piano and they all ask their teachers first for a recommendation for a quality piano tuner. As you can see, this is a very good thing for me as well as for the business owner. They save a ton on their regular piano maintenance and I get a steady stream of loyal customers. Some of my best feeder businesses have my cards and signs displayed prominently in their storefront windows. I provide them with high quality full color signs and printed materials. The time that I work in this feeder network may seem like a sacrifice in immediate income but it is the absolute opposite. Without this network, I would have many less customers every week and make thousands of dollars less every year. It really is true that word-of-mouth advertising is the best and this is a supreme way to leverage word-of-mouth advertising. This simple technique has been a key factor in my ability to double my customer base every year for the past four years. You can apply this feeder network technique to every industry and in many different ways. You should approach it as an "I'll scratch your back if you scratch mine" type of deal. Many business owners understand this type of arrangement and are happy to work with you.

16

High Clients

When you get the chance, do everything you can to work for high visibility clients even if you have to bend over backwards and give extremely crazy deals. Why???? Just take my word for it; it will pay off huge for many years. I was given the opportunity to tune for pop superstar John Legend one summer as he was passing through our town to headline a huge citywide concert. I worked it out with the event management to pay me my regular fee in cash and supply two tickets to the show.

I had to do a little extra work on the piano because I had to arrive 8 hours early to prep and then touch up the tuning right before the concert in front of 5,000 screaming drunken fans in the rain and in the dark. I do work for high-end clients but it is rare in my area (the

Midwest) to tune for a pop culture superstar of this caliber and fame.

I immediately posted pictures of the event on my Facebook page and let my customers know that I was tuning for him that day. I display this on my home page, which shows people that I have tuned for high-end clients. It was a regular tuning like I perform every day for a 9 year old piano student but it sounds much more impressive!

You must grab these opportunities and flaunt them to help people see that you are highly qualified and sought after by the community for your work. Every one of these opportunities will make you a little more recognizable and give you a better resume for the future.

I have tuned pianos for many other famous musicians and TV personalities and I always add them to my list of clients and take pictures when I can. It is important to do this type of work because it will stretch you and give you the experience you need to become the best in your field but regarding public relations and marketing, it is priceless.

17

Credibility

There is a professional organization for almost every niche imaginable. You probably already know about one for your niche. Even if you do, I encourage you to do a good Google search and find out what is out there. For example, there are two main professional organizations for my piano tuning niche. The Piano Technicians Guild (PTG) has about 4,000 members and there are two types of membership that you can obtain. The organization has several regional and a national convention every year and mostly focuses on furthering the education and competence of their membership. They also publish a monthly trade journal and have a nice web site where you will be listed once you become a member.

Most professional organizations provide

online listings and links to their members' web sites. This can boost your web site visibility in major search engines as discussed in previous chapters.

Once you join a trade organization in your niche, you will use their logos and put any credentials that you have acquired by joining these organizations. Always put these logos and credentials high and large on all of your web pages and printed materials (business cards, flyers, letterhead). This works like a constant endorsement and builds the customers' confidence in you adding to your "Know, Like, Trust" factor.

Also, join your local Chamber of Commerce and any other professional organizations with big names and great reputations. Doing this will help build a strong image for your business and help you get more customers!

Compare prices and benefits of each organization. Joining all of them at once could be very expensive. As your business grows you will be able to participate in more organizations and build a strong resume.

If you choose not to join these types of

professional organizations, it will have a negative impact on your image, reputation and your credibility. In short, you will loose money!

I pay about $700 per year to keep my membership in several professional organizations and it pays off every year.

Eric Michael Roberts

18

Recommendations

This simple and free strategy in marketing is highly effective. I can't think of another free marketing strategy that will bring you as much business. When your business shows multiple positive customer reviews it boosts consumer confidence a huge way. If you can't think of where to start, simply begin asking your closest customers or friends to write a review of your services or provide a simple testimonial. Use these blurbs front and center on your web site and create a page where people can email you reviews and testimonials. I asked some of my regular customers to write a review on my Google Plus page and it helped get me a high star rating in Google. This is a very visible online technique for showing people you have a positive business that can be trusted. None of my close competitors have any reviews on their Google page. This makes me look like the best choice when it really counts. To build a strong page of reviews, you have to ask people for reviews. I have never been turned down when I have asked for a review. When I ask for a review, I provide an example from a previous customer so they see exactly what I am looking for. It is best to ask by email or in a Facebook message. When you ask using email or Facebook message, it only takes a few minutes for them to type something nice about you and hit reply. Once you have a good review, you can use it for many years. Try your best to get these types of reviews and recommendations from high visibility clients. For example, I use reviews from local music storeowners and directors from the local performance venues. These look very prestigious and build even more customer confidence.

Always add the person's name and city. Ask the person for permission to put this on your web site. If the testimony is from a high visibility client like a music storeowner, be sure to include their name, position and a link to their web site.

Eric Michael Roberts

19

Hello

When I was in college I started teaching guitar lessons and began to build a large student base. After a few years, I opened my own teaching studio and began to expand my business to include other teachers. At this point, I needed to increase my student base even more. I was teaching so many hours every day that I did not have the time to answer the phone. I was a small startup business so I did not want to pay extra money to hire a secretary so I decided to use a voice mail system. Looking back, I know that it was one of the main causes of my stunted growth. When I became a piano technician I didn't want to repeat this mistake so I now carry a cell phone, even when I am in a customer's home. I answer that phone every time it rings and I get about half of my new customers over the phone. Many business owners feel

too busy to answer the phone or they fail to see the benefit of carrying a cell phone so they are accessible to their customers at all times. Your most loyal customers and those who have been personally referred to you will probably leave a message and patiently wait for you to return their call but the other half will not! They will immediately hang up and call the next business number they can find because most people want instant gratification. They are calling you because they have a need and are ready to spend the money. If you want to increase your business and make profit you must answer the phone. If you can't answer the phone for some reason, be sure to return calls promptly. Use a short and friendly voice mail and use the opportunity to remind customers that they can book an appointment fast and easily at your web site.

20

Remind Them

It is very important to stay in front of your customer at all times! You should constantly be reminding your customer that you are in business and always ready to help. I do this by sending a yearly reminder card. Exactly one year from the last service, my customers receive a post card that reminds them that a year has past and it is a good time to get the piano tuned again. You cannot assume that they have kept your business card and will call when they are ready. My customers need to be reminded that it is time for another tuning. This is similar to the sticker that the auto mechanic places in the upper corner of your windshield. It reminds you that you are way behind on the oil change. Depending on your niche, you may think of other creative ways to remind your customers, but a simple note in the mail is the most reliable method for sending a reminder. I have my reminder post cards printed by an online service such as www.vistaprint.com or www.gotoprint.com. As an example, in the month of August, I simply sort my customers by last service date and print off an address label for all the customers that were serviced last August. Using a modern database and Avery labels, this takes only 3-5 minutes each month and always produces repeat business. My customers rely on my record keeping and diligence to keep them on track with their yearly maintenance. My post card has a small line where I can write the month and year of their last tuning and it always includes a big call to action to BOOK ONLINE! I use snail mail for reliable yearly reminders instead of email because many people change their email address often. I don't want my reminder to land in a spam folder or get sent back. If you want to be sure they get their reminder use the physical mail system. If the postcard is returned to you, you can call them and update the system with their new address. To make this system easy to manage, I include a data field in my customer database labeled "LAST SERVICE". I periodically go through last service date record and send special notes or post cards to customers who have not have their piano serviced in the last 18 months or 2 years. I send a nice letter or special postcard reminding them again that it is important to have regular tunings to keep their piano sounding great.

21

Specialize

When you start you business and begin to communicate to the community that you are open for business it is important that you specialize. I must assume that you are opening a business to fill a need in your community. If there is no need for your service or product, it is going to be extremely difficult or nearly impossible to make a profit and sustain a successful business. Remember that no amount of advertising can create a need. Once you have found a need in your community and have learned how to successfully fill that need you can crank in a profit.

When you are in the act of marketing, you will be focusing all of your attention and resources toward communicating that you are highly qualified to fill a special niche. If you have a lawn care business, you should not also claim that you could install gutters. When you find a profitable niche, work inside that niche and build a great reputation.

When you try to do too many things you tend to spread your resources too thin and you create a confusing message. For example, as a piano technician, I focus on tuning and repairs in my client's home or at performance venues. I can rebuild a piano and will sometimes do this type of work in a slow season but I make most of my income tuning and repairing on site. Other piano technicians focus on rebuilding and have successful rebuilding shops. The skills are very similar but the equipment, space needed, client list and business model are very different.

When I owned a private lesson studio, I also added a small demo-recording studio in my space and added demo production services to my business. Lessons and recording are both music business services but they require very different business models and clients. They also require a different type of space, different kinds of equipment and skills. My recording business was fun and exciting but it dramatically decreased my lesson business because it took up space and time. Startup cost to enter the recording business is very high so it took funds away from my marketing and development of the music lesson business. In the end, I realized that the recording services where hurting the overall business.

It is hard enough to run one aspect of a successful business and communicate that clearly to your community. I always suggest that you specialize in one area where you find the largest need that you can easily fill. You will make great profit running your own business in this manner.

Conclusion

Now it is your turn! Putting all of these techniques to work will take time and dedication. Start by completing your web site and logos and build a strong and professional look for your business. Then, work through each of the other marketing techniques I have shared with you. Theses techniques are designed to be implemented over a long period of time. Used together they will generate a constant flow of new customers for your business. Not a single one of these techniques are meant to work overnight or by themselves. Some will work fast and others will build slowly. Using them all together over time will give you the best results. Tracking your success and watching your business grow is the best reward. Just remember that your business is worth it and your income should steadily increase over time. Thank you so much for reading this book!

If this book has helped you, please take a few minutes to write a quick review and give it a high start rating Amazon.com. I greatly appreciate it! Again, I want to thank you for reading this book and I pray for your great success!!

About the Author

Eric Michael Roberts

Eric is a serial-entrepreneur and independent author. He has a music education degree from Wright State University. Along with a successful local piano tuning service business, he is also the author of the 8 chords 100 songs guitar lesson program and writes books and instructional videos on many topics including music, internet marketing, business development and small business marketing.

http://www.ericmichaelroberts.com

http://www.21bookseries.com

21 Books are a series of books that provides key information such as; tips, facts, ways, how to's, and much more on a wide variety of topics and niches. It is our goal to provide quality content and pertinent information for our readers on almost any topic through quick and easy to read books. Our books are available in a variety of formats such as; e-books, printed, and some are available as audio books. For more information on the many other books that we have available for your reading enjoyment, please visit our website at www.21bookseries.com.

We are a constantly growing company and we are always interested in more books. Are you an expert or highly knowledgeable in a particular subject/niche? If so, have you ever considered writing a book? We provide the resources you will need to make your book a reality. Our website will give you instructions on how to submit your book idea. We would love to hear from you!

Thanks so much for reading this 21 book and remember, "There's 21 for everything!"

http://www.21bookseries.com

www.ingramcontent.com/pod-product-compliance
Lightning Source LLC
Chambersburg PA
CBHW071621170526
45166CB00003B/1142